Must Die

ALSO BY JACOB DAVIES

The Things They've Never Seen (2020)
Every Night is November (2022)

The Dream Must Die

JACOB DAVIES

T

Copyright © 2024 Jacob Davies

Edited by Rhys M.

The moral right of the author has been asserted.

Apart from any fair dealing for the purposes of research or private study, or criticism or review, as permitted under the Copyright, Designs and Patents Act 1988, this publication may only be reproduced, stored or transmitted, in any form or by any means, with the prior permission in writing of the publishers, or in the case of reprographic reproduction in accordance with the terms of licences issued by the Copyright Licensing Agency. Enquiries concerning reproduction outside those terms should be sent to the publishers.

This is a work of fiction. Names, characters, businesses, places, events and incidents are either the products of the author's imagination or used in a fictitious manner. Any resemblance to actual persons, living or dead, or actual events is purely coincidental.

Troubador Publishing Ltd
Unit E2 Airfield Business Park,
Harrison Road, Market Harborough,
Leicestershire LE16 7UL
Tel: 0116 279 2299
Email: books@troubador.co.uk
Web: www.troubador.co.uk

All poems written to be screamed aloud.

ISBN 978 1 83628 071 2

British Library Cataloguing in Publication Data.
A catalogue record for this book is available from the British Library.

Printed and bound by CPI Group (UK) Ltd, Croydon, CR0 4YY
Typeset in 11pt Minion Pro by Troubador Publishing Ltd, Leicester, UK

CONTENTS

PART A

Dear Shauna	3
A Stranger	5
Quarry Hill	8
The Language of Flowers	10
Hugs at the Station	12
Gone Half Past Two	14
Smiling Lovers	16
England	18
Ernie at the Seaside	20
All You'll Want Is to Be Back Here	23
Am I Allowed to Say?	24
She Is the Song	26
Angsty Artist, Circa 2020	28
When You Blurt Out of the Radio	30
Bring the Summer	32
An Ode to You	34
If Madness Meant	39
Table for One	40
The Walk	42
When the Fog Won't Clear	44
My Name	45
Mother of the Accused	46
My Wedding Day	50
There Are Times	52
I Miss Your Mind	54
Coming Home is Terrible	56
A Poem for a Broken Window	57
Frontwoman	58
Friday 16th December	60
Once I Shared a Bed	62

PART B

Not All of Me Is Ugly	65
The Dream Must Die	68
Engaged at Nineteen	70
My Soulmate	72
Liverpool	74
From Heaven to St Helens	75
The Lights Are Off, but Somebody's Home	76
Music Is Your Only Friend	78
Jimmy's a Singer	80
High Town	82
If You Were a Twin	83
Please Read to Me	84
The Brain Gone Stale	85
When I Get Back from the Funeral	86
Think of Me	88
Me and a Friend of a Friend	90
Shake a Spear, My Way	91
20th March	92
In the End There Will Be Silence	94
Si Solo, Amigo	96
What's the Secret?	97
Your Wedding Day	98
Another Day	100
New Year's Eve	102
Shane MacGowan	103
If I Were to Die	104
Eve	106
Ode to Zopiclone	108
For You	109
Hide Away	110
About The Author	112

"One day I will find the right words, and they will be simple."
        Jack Kerouac (1922–1969)

PART A

DEAR SHAUNA

Shauna, you must promise me
That I am next.
With your tooth-led smile of truth
And your flax parachute
Because I'm unsure how much longer I can go on
Without you.

Dear Shauna, please tell me
That you'll remain.
And that you'll be true to
The clouds that move for you
Because all my dreams are painted with
Your emerald hue.

Shauna, you surely know that
My life is over.
One encounter was enough
For you to rip me apart, to call my bluff
As I rolled on rocks with rum
Two hours was enough.

Dear Shauna, you've got to know
What I could be.
With a caring arm around me
In your Ibizan cottage - introspected, free.
What are your plans
This New Year's Eve?

I'm going to be one hundred and four people
Not one of them yours, not one of them real
As I am dual, countless, numerous lives
And only malicious in kind
Explaining the inexplicable
And dying at Springhill
Down, out and thrice counted
Experimentally extraterrestrial mounted
With thoughts like tobacco
And eyes that sink into shadows
Dear Shauna, you must know
My indifference to lies, fame and clichés
So please come and halt the haze
This shameful pattern of my existence.
Dear Shauna, I hang in despair
But you must know, if the offer was there
Dear Shauna in a moment, I would
Follow you twice around the world.

A STRANGER

If I could go back
It's quite curious to think
The times that I'd
Choose to relive.

I'd go to an unfriendly February, an overcast Tuesday
So frosty, so dreary – and so very grey
Where adolescent dreams, tickle the mundane
And young bones groan, for the sunlight to hide away.

If I could go back
I'd eagerly awaken on that nagging weekday,
One that once seemed like a chore
And I'd breathe in every moment
Of what living was like before
They had all gone away
And gone would be
Where they'd stay.

I'd venture out
Into a stirring, shaking Pontefract town
With liquorice fields, and three-pound meal deals
Fuelling a sweet and sour merry-go-round.
If I could go back, I'd sit amongst friends
And see the present in a way only the past can be seen
They would be dystopian days, again of course
But with hindsight, new value I would see.

If I could go back
I'd take in all that nonsense about
Goffman, Marx and Murray
And be far less deliberate, much less eager
For time to fly by, in such a hurry.
I'd laugh with those I cared for again
As the afternoon made itself comfy
And I'd be free. One with secure rain
I'd saviour the air, each instant
Of the moments in time before
We became so distant.

And if I could go back
I'm not sure if I'd go and visit her
But I'd maybe send a fax, or a short text
Via carrier pigeon, without weight or religion
Just to say hello, one final time
Just to reconnect.
Whilst she lived on the same hopeless earth as I
In days before she knew she was
So soon to say goodbye.

And if I could go, to where no one can
Of course, of course, of course, I'd again see you
Waiting for me, with your tentative nature
Slim shadow and jeans duotone blue
If I could go back, to stroll there again
Involuntarily, I'd smile
As my eyes met yours
For the first time, in a short while.

And I'd tell an awkward joke about Ginsberg
Or Coleridge, Keats… or something equally as absurd
And you'd laugh anyway, as if it were
The finest, most brilliant thing you'd ever heard.
And I'd recite a quote or poem – badly, of course
And you'd applaud me and laud me, just because
You were you and I was me, you'd look at me wide-eyed
As the genius that I never was.

If I could go back
I'd seize the day, no danger
Before I knew you were
To become a stranger.

QUARRY HILL

I slogged through the storm, my oh my
At Quarry Hill, that was my life.
Dare I ask why, as I watch my flesh mesh into time?
All of autumn nestles in your hair, whereas I…

Smirked just slightly – upon Normanton bypass
But I swear, no further than that could I laugh.
I'm so easily sold by a smile, you'd only have to ask
To count each regret inside, these given-up, scarlet-shot eyes.
Sail towards these lowly suburbs and you'll know
Anything goes. Anything goes.

I find it very odd – we don't think too often of our heartbeats
Or where we go when we fall asleep.
I don't emerge from darkness but I drown in spite
And somehow each day, you survive, whereas I…

Am on the floor, my oh my
At Quarry Hill, the rain explains the plagues of time
And in every smash, I hear each minor note, I feel the bite
Of the soundtrack of my life.

…

But I'm sure once you looked in my boyish blue eyes
And I…
Didn't feel such pain, upon the lap of that delight.

And now I, my oh my, must come and go with time
Watch me! Watch me! See me, pass by…
Too late.

I swear you pitied the surprise of my continuous sighs
And I…
Couldn't even utter the word goodbye, that night.
I'm always only a moment away from my demise
Watch me! Watch me! See me, pass by…
Always too late.

Across the streets I swept as God wept, my oh my
At Quarry Hill, I dropped to the pavement that night
Huge problem, I might even love you and I'm
Not entirely sure of anything, that's mine
Anymore.

THE LANGUAGE OF FLOWERS

I don't belong.
Where daffodils wait until
William's been and gone.

I don't belong.
I'm on the mend, I now only spend
Tuesdays in the shed.

What do friends look like?
Carnations seem to know their faces
And all the days they've wasted.

I still don't belong.
I sob and I cry, as bluebells die…
Mozart was born and gone by thirty-five.

He drifted from Vienna
And then soon, he forever
Frowned in the ground
Aside orchids, soil and me.
Snowdrops sang, and now I am,
Neither land, nor sea.

Sunflowers, take an hour
Whilst marigolds hold my soul

And beg me that I go.
Buttercups, never shut up
And daisies say far too much
Just like me, they've had enough.

No tulips
Could pout my two lips
Or poppy, stop me… on my decline.

Lily is lost in the valley.
Chrysanthemums, have left me numb
So naive, and so very young.

Dorothy Parker knows
One perfect rose
Cannot, for money be bought or sold.
As there, time froze!
Forget-me-nots, don't remember
They do not know
The wandering of my ghost.

HUGS AT THE STATION

Hugs at the station
From a star-crossed lover, or a belt-blazing mother
Partner through sedation, or spellbound relation
And I watch.

Smiles near the trains
Between husband and wife, fork and knife
Couples in love strange, without shame, yet to be estranged
And I ponder.

Chuckles from nearby seats, through the telephone
Not a chord of pretend, the voice at the other end
They think, they're so sure they know, embodies a safe and happy home
And I wonder. What is this like?

Shoes scuttle side by side on the station floor
Stations across nations, Cork, Paris, New York
I find it hard to ignore, I shall never have closure for
All the lives we dreamt of having.

Far-off accents by the railway
Make me smile blue, they remind me of you
I remember how I stayed, and off you went away
And I carry that with me.

Goodbye! – they tearfully beam.
See you soon! – they say grinning, swimming through
The dissipation of an afternoon
The depletion of
Their whole lives!
And my heart bleeds for noon.
And my heart bleeds for them.
And my heart bleeds for you.
My heart.
Bleeds.

GONE HALF PAST TWO

On some nights, the streetlights
Are more blatant than on others.
They illuminate what, you'd much rather not
Have seen, have shown.
They're an open broadcast of the forlorn.

What shape is the hole inside you?
How soon, how soon, how soon
Will your voice be eaten by time?
Forgotten. Drained.
Withdrawn by the practicality of the existential.

Shimmering, glistening, rambunctious riot of night
Because without what makes
Your hallowed eyes blue
You feel completely at one with each
Of your worst days…

All I'm saying is
I might not necessarily get up
In the morning.

Streetlight glares at 2am
And carves your secluded soul open
As she is lifted to ecstasy
As if you never existed
Carried to the trance of happy inebriation

By the lady who'll always be a stranger
To you.

And who are you?
Just another human being
Slowly dying
Still looking at the streetlights
At gone half past two.

SMILING LOVERS

Smiling lovers, are all around
Sitting on park benches
With cigarettes.
Or with hands clasped, half-cut
Pretending what they have, is enough.

Smiling lovers, are all around
Under New York Christmas lights
Life trite and trousers too tight
Inventing quirks, and shooting fireworks
A façade to hide a lifelong dirge.

And who am I?
But a child, still with a watchful, alert eye
On what isn't, the many lives fate wouldn't try
And what might've been.

Joyful lovers, on the ground
Rolling fields, rolling eyes; sharing woes
Resentment only grows, and how bluntly it shows
Arguing around shopping centres, market stalls
What the hell is the point of it all?

Joyful lovers, have lost and found one another
Silently reminiscing their lives, before they'd met
Indulging in perpetual, sweet dreams.
Where smiling sunsets are forever drawn
And death comes like a dawn.

And what am I?
But a man, on his way to die
Unwilling to try, so sick of the lie
And completely, entirely, alone.

Tell me what has become of my life?
You'd think I would know better
Than to ask such a question
But please, just pop the answer in a letter
To the padded cell, that is my home address
The one with the great lakes and greater shakes
The padded cell, with the stained rose wallpaper and
The occasional earthquake
Surely it will reach me…
Surely?

Tell me what has become of tonight?
You'd think I would, by now, know better
Than to tempt fate
But please, make the trip a little later
To the padded cell, where I reside
The one with the old wooden sign… *here lies, happier times*
The padded cell, with the pretty flowers, leisure half-an-hours and
Where the patients whisper lonely goodbyes, to the saline tune
Of hourly funeral chimes
Surely you will reach me…
Surely?

ENGLAND

From the rooftop beer garden with the broken vent
To your safe and warm Yorkshire bed
Via the wake in the snug bar, life is always in two halves.
Follow your heart as far as Boston Spa, and you'll see
Soho musings of Blake and young Morrisseys
Terraced houses filled with sardonic slurs
Coronation Streets and back-bedroom casualties
Words filled with angst, piss and vinegar.

I know you are far from untouchable, and for a start
I am sick to death of blue and red politicians and
You can shove your British beef up your arse
But I see past the mirrors and smoke, I see the glorious parts that make you whole
And when I sing with your air, I know I am home.
In cities and countryside, both yours and mine
The Royal Exchange, rented rooms in Whalley Range
Are familiar and friendly in their charming ways.

Accents in Manchester, Leicester, Liverpool, Leeds
Lucy in the sky and Julie in the weeds
Actors and singers in figures of eights
Last-minute winners, indie bars on Briggate
Sundays sheltered by fireside, from undetermined sleet
The humming glow and golden trickle of streetlights on our English streets
Cathedrals and history, real heritage and tradition
Powerful men, powerful women, and acoustic admissions.

Foot to cobbled pavement, and up shoots
A strength in my stride, and pride in my English roots
And though generations have failed you, in slander and shame
My heart treasures my own definition of your name.
There is no doubt, you have done wrong
But the future is pure, and we will be fine
England, I love you. I am yours
And you are mine.

ERNIE AT THE SEASIDE

Ernie, a boy of just nine years, went on a trip to the beach
His grandparents on the pier, holding a hand of his each
They ambled, rambled – half a mile
As summer was, the light flowing smile
Of the waves trickling by his feet.

Ernie was sad the day had to end, he wanted it to go on forever
But handing the boy a paper bag, grandfather's plan was clever
Ernie took a toffee; a sweet, and another, and another
And in the back of the car, he turned and asked his grandmother…
Will life be this joyful forever?

The boy held curiosity, as Grandma placed a hand on his cheek
As softly she said, *we are here to provide memories, that you will forever keep*
And as day turned to evening, the grandmother smiled
Country road yards turned to motorway miles
And Ernie drifted off to sleep.

Time went by, as it often tends to
Ernie became older, new focuses, new things to do
Grandmother, grandfather… waited at home, far from despair

Contented and pleased with the times together they had shared
As Ernie ventured on eras anew.

The world's vibrant fruits, began to fade to black
Health waned, and fate won its attack
Ernie watched his grandmother die
And his grandfather cry
Desperate to have a childhood seaside day back.

Ernie, half a man now, went on a trip to the beach
Echoes the only answer – such distress he'd beseech
With grief to pay a lifelong debt
As time was the salty, chilly wet death
Of the waves biting at his feet.

Ernie, distraught and starved of joy,
Trudged through the years, to search and to destroy
But soon, fortune spun his way
And one sunny day
Ernie was a father, of a girl and a boy.

They'd gain years of their own, twenty-seven – and counting – each
No matter the mistakes he'd make, or lessons he'd try to teach
And one day, sure enough, rang the telephone
Ernie had grandchildren of his own
It was time for a trip to the beach.

A wonderful day was enjoyed by all at the beach
Ernie's elderly arms on the pier, a grandchild in each
But on the way home, the words the infants said
Brought an ancient memory, back to Ernie's head
With juvenile curiosity, they smiled and asked, *Grandad,
　will happy times always be in reach?*

And as the granddaughter held curiosity, Ernie began to speak
I am here to provide memories, that you will forever keep
And, as grief turned to joy, the grandfather smiled
Country road yards turned to motorway miles
And the children drifted off to sleep.

ALL YOU'LL WANT IS TO BE BACK HERE

Down again flies the angsty sun
You are miserable and ugly, but young
And all you'll ever want
Is to be back here.

Your parents are alive, for now
And so are you – God knows how
One day, you'll pledge and you'll pray to give it all away
To be back in this moment.

Up again slogs the tired sun
You are lonely and holy, but still half drunk
The frustration, the elation, the joy
To have not yet been born.

Change will come, much sooner than you think
No matter how well you can hide or resist
You'll beg for time to reverse, to redisperse
All that you have lost.

Up shoots the bullet of the moon
You are pure of mind and so full of gloom
And one day, all you'll ever want
Is to again be here
And again, be you.

AM I ALLOWED TO SAY?

Crisp and moody grey skies
Settle calmly, and harmonise the devil's eyes
Here, as the slow caution of dusk embraces the moon
Am I allowed to say…?

Lovely blackening skies, made for goodbyes
Eliminate the glass pretence of flagrant butterflies
I fly the flag for the disappearing afternoon
Am I allowed to say…?

Mid-morning white paint and clinical skies
I told the usual lie, I said everything was fine
My head spins a tail, and tames a shrew
Am I allowed to say…?

Off run hours, sinking drinks that taste like
Knowing where summer goes and a lost dog's breath on ice
Fraught, tired – sending days back to June
Am I allowed to say…?

The next thing to kill us all, awakes from the mud
Because nothing at all in life, comes to any good
And yet,
I can still see my fate in your face, a spluttering of sighs
I think, at last I know why I stayed alive
And so, can I speak what is true?
Am I allowed to say…?

Hand me a card, an emergency number to escape trouble
Where after 7pm the calls cost double
And yet,
Even as I am… strapped to the bench; fixated on the shelf
I could as soon forget myself
As to forget you.
Am I allowed to say…?

Time has hardened the softer edges
And drawn my wandering eyes towards high window
   ledges
And yet,
You seem to complete all
The silly half ideas in my head
But I avoided the question the first time
And I shall do so again.

SHE IS THE SONG

Time was once a lover
A companion of mine, aside
Behind – or somewhere nearby
As days become garments, that are shapeless… marked
She is the song.

She is the song
Of moments not short, nor long
Immaculately balanced – timed, a glance
A smirk-turned-laugh
Held in seconds, that I treasure.

Rise of sickly dawn was once a charm
My legs can only carry me so far
In suspicion of optimism
And awe of how, eternally, forevermore
She is the song.

She is the song
In the ashes of my life
Wormhole, galactic eyes
To explore, to conquer… to fall for
Fall into and die.

Second guesses and silent confessions
Confusion and quite
Possible delusion – naivety and incredulity
She has forged in my mind
She is the song.

She is the song.
The break from all rotten, all callous
All wrong, all gone…

She is the song.

I know, nothing more.

ANGSTY ARTIST, CIRCA 2020

Angsty artist,
With a record spinning on your turntable
And your knitted cardigan sleeves rolled
Halfway up.
Pondering if
Your time alive can be defined by poetry
As there are words you cannot find that
Would mean so much to me.

Starved artist,
With your hair styled like your idol's
Scratching quotes onto a page, while all
The subjects live their lives.
Wondering why,
Books, whisky, tear-filled eyes
And golden streetlights on rainy nights
Make you feel the way they do.

Are you enriched or bewitched,
By the passing of your life?
Unsure if
You're gaining or losing so very much
From each night that lives and then dies.

'Crying Lightning'
Swirls out of the speakers
Because you only want to be like the people
Who've become their truth.
Questioning if
It's worth just giving in
Or if a loveless life is worth it for
The great nothing you've achieved.

Are you content or are you spent,
Living on the outskirts of the present?
Never sure if
You're gaining or losing anything
From your despair that is so frequent.

Brooding artist,
Carving and whittling an identity
That outside of your mind doesn't exist.
Rachmaninoff isn't enough,
To quench your soul's thirst
Because you're in agony too
The perpetual pain of life fuels you
You carry it around everywhere you go
You feel it in everything you do.

Angsty artist,
I think of you broken hearted
For your uncertainty is precious
You've got the message, for sure
But you're not sure if you're
The messenger.

WHEN YOU BLURT OUT OF THE RADIO

As England aches to return
Crows gather one by one
To taunt me with murmurs, skull to gun
As Escapril packs up magnanimous, I am stunned
But your song spits out of the radio
And our lives drip on.

And as I
Travel from illiterate to literary gem
And then very swiftly back again
As I
Wrestle and hassle to become doe-eyed by
A certain type of romance, I
Hear your resurrection via waved projection.

When you blurt out of the radio
You cut through
The perpetual sequence of disillusion
My heart is unable to become accustomed to
I am awake.

And as I
Make several studded, full-blooded pearl necklaces
From incoming Monday nights and second guesses
As I

Try to break the stone slate on my face and veins
And unpack the rocks clouding my brain
I feel the second coming of your grace.

When your song cannonballs from the radio
The mouth-open awestruck, infantile look, reappears
The sea and the land, does what it can
But my mind only sings, when you lunge here
I am alive.

When your song creeps from the speaker
A sprit appears, from the dust
And the people here don't even notice
The sound of your words, they're not like us
They're nothing at all like us.

And as your
Delicate song crashes out of the radio
I know what I am
Again.
When you appear in words and melody
Judge me or love me
Sedate me or hate me but
Here I am again,
The poet's sun shall bite back
Against the rain.

BRING THE SUMMER

Bring the summer
The full-bodied, spotless scent of freshly cut grass
Bring the loving summer and
We'll leave the past in the past.

Bring the summer
Yorkshire fields adorned by eight o'clock sunsets
Bring the boisterous summer with
Sun-kissed beers and mousy hair, windswept.

Bring the summer
Let it be the remedy
To silly situations of adoration
I invent in my head.
Bring the summer and
Let me feel free.

Bring the summer
With verse so simple, it's clever
Bring the bonny summer and
Make it last forever.

Bring the summer
How the evening slightly chills
Bring a tempestuous summer and
Cure this child ill.

Bring me summer, or even
Late April will do.
Bring me summer, bring it soon
Bring me summer
And make sure you're there too.

AN ODE TO YOU

Look, look, look at me.
Look, look, look at me.
When you are half awake,
Or even half asleep.

Upon the moment I first saw you,
I wanted to assess, to trail your coat all day
If you were to come back here,
For just a little while, I'd say…

I have written an ode to you
I hope you don't find it awkward or crude
My life is
An ode to you.

Look, look, look at me.
Look, look, look at me.
With this gift I have possessed
I'll never be bored again.

Upon a lunchtime I saw you after a while,
It was another sunny day.
I wanted to touch your arm,
Wander over and sincerely say…

I have written an ode to you
I hope you don't find it awkward or crude

But my life is
An ode to you.

Upon a landslide we almost crossed paths, again
I'll admit, I went a little out of my way
To engineer our intersection by a lucky turn of fate
I wanted to look into your soul and say…

I have written an ode to you
I hope you don't find it awkward or crude
My life is
An ode to you.

And on that evening, placed by the mouth; upon my bonnet,
You planted a Molotov cocktail and left me frail, draped to hang
As unsubtle as affection, or as the long crawl home,
My senses inside, spun and sang…

I have written an ode to you
I hope you don't find it awkward or crude
But my life is
An ode to you.

Look, look, look at me!
Choking on misery…

Look, look, look at me!
I'd much rather be…

Drowning in the warmth, of your lovely
British, Midlands accent
For which, I am handsomely enamoured
In the purest, truest sense.

Look, look, look at me!
I'd much rather be…

Wading through an afternoon, with you
Slyly, shyly, making innuendo
Nothing sinister or vulgar, just steady
Flirtatious and gentle.

Look, look, look at me!
I'd much rather be…

Where we speak only in verse,
And the lines I write are not only mine
But yours.
Where we beat the traverse,
And the lines I scream are not just bleak
But more.

Look, look, look at me!
I'd much rather be…

In a trailer, fashionably paler
Amidst the art and lure of your olive skin
Where Pablo Neruda is not only on the page
But in every heartbeat of the life, we are within.

Look, look, look at me!
I'd much rather be...

In the world where I am the man to say
Look, look, look at me!
Look at me, my wonderful life
And dazzling story.

Look, look, look at me!
I'd much rather be...

Where we speak only in verse,
And the lines I write are not only mine
But yours.
Where we are contractually perverse,
And to you, my face is not just an acquainted crime
But adored.

Look, look, look at me!
I'd much rather be...
In a world where I can say...

Look, look, look at me!
Look, look, look at me!
Look at me, my wonderful life
And our unified story!

Look, look, look at me!
I'd much rather be...
In a world where I can say...

I have written an ode to you
I hope you don't find it awkward or crude
My life is
An ode to you.

And if I am to drift and float away,
And if I am to wander and go away,
Don't you dare make me stay.
Don't even think of asking me to stay.

And if I am to silently weep,
And if I am to die in my sleep
Don't wonder what became of me
Don't even look at me
If I am to die in my sleep,
That is where I'll be.

IF MADNESS MEANT

If madness meant I was
To be with you
I don't mind being slightly
Out of my mind.

If madness meant you were
To dictate my days
Doctor, go on – I'm so ready
Drag me away.

And if my life was to
Evolve unsolved and
Separate from your sureness
I'll be here always.

And
If madness meant life would
Give a little more than I first thought
In absurdity, I am all yours,
For escape out of the back door is
A fate far worse.

TABLE FOR ONE

Table for one
Now that you have gone
Would it be inadvisable or unwise
To cower towards the colour of absent eyes?

Table for… table for one
They glance my way as if I am the one
Who is simply mad, in solitude
I close my eyes and see myself hang. If only they knew.

I cannot stomach for much longer, the laughter of groups
Have they not grasped, have they simply ignored what is true?
Table for… table for… table for one
Now that you have gone.

Table for one
I am breathing easily, I am a lucky one, on
A park bench, thrust into a generation, soul alone
Communication has dwindled to its death, curse the telephone.

The memory is fading, of what it was to have you near
Each place I go, the song of your spirit disappears
Through distant idle talk, new and relevant conversations
That can no longer take place, due to old revelations.

Table for… table for one
My life has scuttled, scurried, hurried on
Circle now, finished. Sadly complete
Spinning around on these spinning streets,

And exploring brand new
Dead-end, broken-promise avenues
From the start until the end of us. I was unseen.
So, what is it worth? What did it all mean?
Table for, table for…
The done and the undone.
And the plans we made
Have faded away,
To oblivion.

My heart wandered off, sometime ago
No use, no use, for your amicable theft
And truly, trust me – there's nothing cathartic
About your own lonely death.

THE WALK

The walk was a little longer than I remembered.
Trees overgrown; weather phased from pure to dreary
To snoozy and clear
Rocks below are jagged and stoned; I'm starting to forget to remember,
What it was like to have you near.

Ornamental carpet grass, turned to crisp macabre ash
Hemlocks gone; weeds aplenty
Graffiti spat and sprawled onto bridge walls, spoke and said,
Here we were, in brutal 2020.

The walk was a lot quieter than I remembered.
The sky aimed to taunt – rung out dry, like a wet rancid towel
My footsteps, were crisp yet quiet
My lungs, wished to howl.

The canal scoped, scanned and ran on, further than I thought.
Dewdrops of hope inside me stretched out, smoothly strung
From some to naught
And then soon, from naught to none.

The bridge was slightly thinner than I remembered.
I looked at the water below lustfully, I wanted to haul myself off
The remorseless, insatiable devil in my mind spoke clearly,
And told me all the reasons why I should not.

The sun slowly settled as I walked.
Is it the last time I'll see it here? Who knows.
There is no way to bandage up… provide first aid to
These open, ferocious, wounded woes.

I hope they never find the walk I went on, the places I've been
The trees, the leaves, the sweet marine-dusted scent of herbs,
Obliterated when they discover it, destroyed wholly and forever
With their ignorance and their silly, bitter words.

The walk was a lot longer than I had recalled.
Than how it used to feel, in the spring… the summer
As I walk again, tears appear… they sneer upon my senses
Heart heavier,
Heart fuller.

WHEN THE FOG WON'T CLEAR

Somewhere out of tune, out of time
When the fog won't clear
Somewhere in my mind, a certain kind
In a different sphere, a future year
Stalling in a different gear.

Somewhere out of place, out in space
When the mist won't resist
Somewhere drifting towards sleep, in peace
With pity, my face faintly kissed
And gradually less missed.

And you'll fetch me my final meal
As you did my very first
I'll close my eyes, I shall pause my tears
As I try to recollect, all that I was
And all that we were.

MY NAME

Simple syllables and words uttered
By my father and by my mother
When I was small and uncluttered
Raw, vulnerable, curious.

My name, they would say
And I'd respond – half in vain
For I believed the world was made
Of shoelaces and magic.

My name, you once confessed
In a breeze of birdsong and loveliness
Before fate and I made such an awful mess
A song in a pocket.

I squint upon my reflection and I say
My name, as desensitisation fades away
I realise, I am I – tomorrow and today
Such a weight.

Tonight, I am introduced by name
Not as the headline, I earnestly step on stage
To fire back, eyes-locked, at those who watch and to say
All that I must.

My name, they will eulogise
With dry, teary or glazed-over eyes
I must confess it has come with surprise
To discover the sorry meaning, of my sorry life.

MOTHER OF THE ACCUSED

Steadily, she angled her bed
And westwards, rested her head
Sinking body drops; legs gently fall
Six and a half inches from the floor…

Seven months gone and
Forever to go
Love has lost the frivolous infancy I'm
Not sure it ever had.

Seven months gone and
Away went the snow
Branwell Brontë got to know me
But never loved me.

I am Sarah Russell's third life
You have so many friends
How am I supposed to
Compete with them?

I am auditioning for a part
In a film noir
I'm not ready for a renaissance
Not ready, never ready.

Speaking in 'S's
And plotting confessions
As he falls apart
I do too.

You take the stand
And I am Exhibit A; the 2nd of May
2021… yesterday and tomorrow
Have quickly come and gone.

Seems so long ago
Seems so… very long ago.
All thoughts, physically
Hold the same weight.

An age when birthdays
Are not about looking forward
But looking back
Three cheers for the life you didn't have.

Why not? It didn't come to you and
You didn't go to it
The joke's not as funny
When I do it.

The Foreman is in the woods
He plays in a band
But they're
Not very good.

*They strut about singing
Teenage kicks
With Rohypnol and
Expensive drumsticks.*

*But of course,
All gold turns to rust
As he fades to dust,
I do too!*

*People swerve me
For all the right reasons
And faith is a curse
If you can believe it.*

*If you have any belief at all
Follow me*
Some psychologist, you are.
*If you have any faith in tomorrow –
Just follow…*

Do you think I am
A woman?
No.
I am only
The delirium
Of your loneliness…

Do you think I am
Sylvia Plath?
No.
I am only

The last sign of madness
Gone rotten.

Do we know what time
The postman is due?
I heard on the news
Christmas is supposed to be
Coming soon.

Let me sleep for a moment
For I have travelled so far
Let me rest my head on your lap
And think of all
I'll never have.

Let me die for a while
England, give me warmth
Tomorrow can wait
With its curse and taunt
Let me rest my head on your lap
And dream of all
That we could've had.

Do you think I am
Human?
How mistaken
You appear to be.
I am only the implication
Of the woes you thought
Long ago
You'd shaken.

MY WEDDING DAY

More citalopram than man
I stand here as whatever I am
Find me in a ripped-up
Polaroid picture.

A man with a flat cap gives
A slow hand clap
My life is in ruins, no longer
A Shropshire lad.

Name that tune and I'll
Propose to you
A lifetime apart
And a cleaner for the heart.

How fucking depressing
Would this place be
With the lights on?
Twilight gripes on and on and on…

My wedding day
I am the spirit of your grandmother
And your disappointment of a son
All rolled into one…
Hip-hip, hooray.

My wedding day
This must be how it feels to have won
Fulfilment, happiness, joy
Add up to none
Hip-hip, hooray.

Receiving the grant
Of good fortune, well wishes
From your simple, silly aunt
God, kill me.

Dear precious, precious hell
Of time and its sketchy spell
To remove and reuse darkness at will
God, end me…
Finish me…
End me…

…

It seems to me, you aim
All of your life
To be inscrutable, complex
Byronically attractive
And so, the very idea that someone could have
Discovered. Solved. Conquered.
And moved on…
Is the greatest devastation imaginable.

Congratulations.

THERE ARE TIMES

There are times I can't think
Of anything at all to live for
At times I recognise that
Most people are awful.

There are times I believe I can
Tie it all together
When the right song comes on
And I write something clever.

There are times I need Jesus
To burn off my skin, to cleanse these sins
To explain, to frame and to sedate
The state I am in.

There are times I'm simply clinging on
And I just want to go home
At times I feel
Completely on my own.

There are occasions I notice
A twinge in my chest and a disconnect
Because of thoughts and flirtations
I have once again forgotten to forget.

There are times I can be played as a tambourine
And life is no longer my own
At times, as you know, I feel
Completely alone.

I MISS YOUR MIND

The last time there was a leap year
We were just beginning
Spring was a song.

Since you went, I quite often hear
Gunshots in my head
Summer is a worry.

I'm not bitter, but
I'm not sure I've ever loved
We are all caught in the waves
Of escaping identical days.

I'm not as naive as I was, I'm aware now
I am the protagonist of a Kaufman film
I can feel each tired line I wrote in this town
Roses follow me around.

I'm not stupid, I know
There is no way out, no shelter
I'm so often trapped by the nausea
Of feeling safe and settled and warm and…

I'm no victim, of course
I know what's right and what's wrong
For you and for me. I run on lies, heartbreak
And peppermint tea.

The next time there is due to be an eclipse
How much more will I be, than still this
Grieving monsoon in a costume?

The next time the moon rises, and again I kill, will I still
Miss your presence, and your mind
As much as I do?

COMING HOME IS TERRIBLE

After *Bonedog* by Eva H.D.

Start each day with a black coffee
And a cigarette from the night before
See yourself as disillusioned, fooled or fuelled
And for the first time, understand fully who you are.

Refuse to move to anyone's tune
For no poet nor fool could teach you a lesson
Spend the day in national museums and in colosseums
And then break again, ready for the evening session.

You haven't given up hope just yet
But you're sure you will soon
For time always fades, and your home always waits
As the drag and trap of a recognised cocoon.

You return, and stop for a moment, in the face of
Familiar silence. Traffic tippling, tongue-twisted, toast burnt
You feel again the crushing weight of lonely bones
And begin to wonder if you ever weren't.

A POEM FOR A BROKEN WINDOW

Could you ever begin to know
The dusky, light-chasing echoes
That leap in the valley of my soul?
With all the militia of your
Unsure, delighted smile
Pity-filled eyebrows that plunge half a mile
Zested with wishes, *all the very best*
Fortified by bartering jargon and
Eyes emergency-siren inflamed, yet
With the fire inside quenched
Could you possibly contest…
The expanse, the expense of what I've become
Unfolding into arms that slip away, and never hold
Rolling into foreign streets, distant and alone.

FRONTWOMAN

The Broken Chains are due on stage
Tame sound, shite name
As always, time dictates
It grows anxiously late.

The hour when some people are going to bed
And others are starting to get up
At last, the lights drop and the chatter stops
And from the darkness emerges, all I knew not.

There she is - the frontwoman
As delicate and as light as a raindrop
She catches my sights and
My tomb appears before my eyes.

The frontwoman, in 2024
As the answer to post-punk, she roars
Draped in a St George's cross tank-top
And for words, sense and verse I am lost.
Her wavy, hurricane hair is a rebellion
Of men in suits and centrist truths
Her teeth snarl through each line and all the while
I forget about you.

She's not afraid to kick out
Nor reluctant to stamp on your head
Because she's enraged, with a war to wage
And she's a feminist.

She's stoned, too amused and opioid infused
And my newest new muse
I have been stirred, and sometimes
You don't need words
Because tonight, I could die
Wrapped up by your eyes
And I wouldn't mind
Too much.

...

At the close of the night
The streets are calm, there's nobody around
Again alone, again unknown - blah blah blah
And by the frontwoman, I am unfound.

And I despair at the thought
That you and this gritty, sickly reality
Is the best that I can do
I slur towards the disappearing hordes
And beseech the silent streets
I ask to her
Where are you? Where are you?
My stride is unsteady, but I'm aware of the answer
I'm in full knowledge of what is true.

FRIDAY 16TH DECEMBER

It begins and it ends
With sin, and with friends
But since you ask, the answer is yes.
My funeral is happening whilst I
Am still alive.

Approach the night with a knowing smile
And leave clutching
A furious aptitude for crying.
Underprepared, freshly repressed
And crudely overdressed.

And one says to another, *oh, how I love you so*
Surely you know, they won't be here tomorrow?
Or through any of the hell
Any pockets of the future, soon to come
Any of the forever that will follow.

I know.

The music sounds… quite good
Don't listen to the lyrics or you'll
Swiftly sober up.
And be sliced by each diatribe
Tomorrow is an enigma to be worked out in your mind.

Before you can breathe, your life starts – eyes must stay sharp
Observing the illuminated dark
We could all be that happy
If we put our souls
Up for sale.

The real nasty story
Shall stay under bolt, lock and key
Alas, *dream of me...* and welcomed by a goodbye
With a kiss on the cheek
Put away, to sleep.

Goodnight.

And what comes with the rise of the day?
Chapters new, ripe emotions that just won't fade away
My memory shall saunter overboard
Released, dropped and washed
Quickly to be no more.

ONCE I SHARED A BED

Once I shared a bed
With you, my soul bled
Out emotions with notions, not dissimilar
To jumping from the church spire.

Once I shared a bed
With a clinging, grasping memory of moments just ahead
Why has nobody noticed that I
Have completely lost my mind?

Once I shared a bed
With wings trimmed, before a chance to spread
Into a twirling world of eye-lock unity and
Footsteps synchronised, hand in hand.

Once I shared stale bread
With an illusion that grasped and scratched at my hairless head
With dreams intertwined and kites flying by
The Shakespearean shade of these houses.

Once I shared my head
With grey-less sky, with clouds that cry instead
Flirting verses of powder and lines of karaoke
Youth is rarely pure, and never simple.

Once I shared a bed
With you, I wept and yes
I said
Of how, even now
After twenty years of stained-glass lies
I still wonder why…

I sleep life off, cold – untouched and overthrown
Deposed and set in stone
And why my thoughts are baron, unshared, yet my fears are
Expertly, Michelin-star prepared
And why my face and groans are depended on
By nobody's bones
And why nightly taxi journeys roll home,
Always quiet, always alone.

PART B

NOT ALL OF ME IS UGLY

Why for as loud as I shout
Do I never hear a reply, nor echo?
And why, for as hard as I try
Is there still so much further to go?

Because not all of me is ugly
I am a long-distance runner with a bell jar
Not all of me is ugly
You're told to be yourself, until the moment you are.

Why do I still bother to dream
Of a place to rely, an existence to acclaim?
And why must I travel, unravel, toil and spoil
To only go back to from where I came?

Because not all of me is ugly
I'm not in love and I spew out like a sore thumb
Not all of me is ugly
Despite the bones I am built from, and all I've done.

Stop the press, halt the news
Stop all the clocks, for I cannot muse
Upon your character assassination, I dry heaved through
To find a million disclosures, I already knew.

Not all of me is ugly
Imprinted and marked by yesterday's fetters and chains

The world is such an uncomfortable place
And I fear you feel the same.

Why am I most certainly uncertain – to be sure
Of what I am and what I am to become?
And why with absolutely nothing left
Do I still seethe on?

I spend my time out of your arms, aside open fires
Open letters and Freudian slips
And cuckoo-nest deniers
Not all of me is ugly
Slumping around as each different man
Taxi drivers think I am.

I spend my life on balconies with Bacardi
With a pissed-off expression and half-lit cigarette
And a less than flattering cardi
But not all of me is ugly
Despite what to you, might be apparent
Many others have surrendered, melted by society. I haven't.

I pass the time inside the sanitised room I was consigned
And I draw your face on the Etch A Sketch
Most of the day and all of the night
Not all of me is ugly
I scribe my cries, in plasma on the walls
I jump to you, and again on my face I fall.

I spend my life cracking wise, aside empty seats
I've never been a baritone

But tediously, I must repeat
Not all of me is ugly
So, sit back with your notebook; take a closer look
Drink orange wine, analyse and scrutinise my actions
My mannerisms, deliriums, and shade-may experiences
Tell me I am forbidden and flog me to the lowest bidder
See the pointless refrains
Of my rip-flagged skin and my mud-dragged name.

But not all of me is ugly
I fear you are just the same.

THE DREAM MUST DIE

I was once positive, that most things
In life could change
And that summer would bring
The solution, and a release from the rain.
But I have seen joy cease, purpose run dry
Perhaps it's time
We should mourn those still alive.

Once in the morning, I sipped union larger
With a taste of honey
And I thought of charging further,
Ambition, and other notions just as funny.
But a truth soon emerged
From just one half-glance at the world,
The dream must die.

The dream to see my words on blessed pages
And my shaking legs on higher stages
The dream to swim in seas
Of those who truly love me
The dream to succeed, to win, to sing
To be or not to be anyone or anything
The dream to live in fame
To have any weight to my name
To be lost and found
And duly lost again
The dream to pause and wait for the rise of the moon

The dream to ever meet you.
The dream must die.

I was once, like you, a child
Wrapped up in the naivety
Of sunshine, comfort and smiles
Of inviting daybreak in April, May and June
But soon came the gloom
The revelation of after the afternoon
That there could be only one answer to.

And so, the dream must sigh
Go sheet-white and die
The dream must cease to breath
And scream out the name of the final faces it sees
If I am to survive, the dream has to die
I feel the shackles of my waking life
They're shaking me awake and pulling me down
Dragging my eyebrows south to frown
And I'm jealous of nobody's life
Because I'm not so sure yet if I even want mine
And so, I say in resignation and in fight
In a low voice turned high
The dream must die.

Let the dream die
This charade must stop
These dreams of mine
Must die.

ENGAGED AT NINETEEN

Engaged at nineteen
Don't you find it all so embarrassing?
Your life beckoned and you let it go
It was once yours for the taking, don't you know?

Engaged at nineteen
Won't you let yourself be happy?
Why not try, give it a go. It isn't easy, I should know – I've been
Chucked around, since the day I turned sixteen.

But you're engaged at nineteen, in the Travelodge hotel bar
Be honest with yourself,
Did you mean for the self-harm
To go quite this far?

Take my advice and save your own life
And make some time
To write these wrongs
Onto paper or into song
Before it's gone, save your own life
And burn all the bridges, you once thought ought
To have been built.

Engaged at nineteen and
That is all you are. You are solely, only a dream of chivalry
Glimpses of moonbeams, half-melted vanilla ice creams
Anecdotes that never end, and second-hand tiger jeans.

Enraged at twenty-three with quaint, paint-tasting metaphors
Half-strung, paracetamol-tongue
Craving just fifteen minutes of anonymity!
A place in hell to go and rest, without a fight or a family
There's such trouble inside
Those wide hazel eyes.
Engaged at nineteen
I have the answer and it's so easy…

Save your kids from being born
And don't bother
Falling in love, because it's all a big con
It's such a lie.
It'll suck you in and call you nice things
It'll make you play shite music
Forget who you are and your reasons to be human
It'll make you paint your face and inspire such senseless whims
Destroy your mind and snap your heartstrings.

Save your own life
Just as I have saved mine.
Dethrone and stone the only one you know
Save your life and
Break your own heart
It's never too late to start
To run away; to tell them you're never coming back
And to become someone
Who you justly love.

MY SOULMATE

꽃

My soulmate is in a Buddhist temple in Japan
They're not fully sold on the idea, unsure how much zen they can stand
My soulmate hangs around outside Los Angeles disco shows
With a lisp, a spliff and shady Jo, who nobody dares to know
My soulmate is not here. I am on my own.

My soulmate is buried in a brickyard
In cement rests their bad decisions, surrounded by stolen equipment
My soulmate is considering getting a Nectar card
But isn't quite ready to make the commitment
Do you see what I am trying to say?

My soulmate died in 1964, in Vietnam
With a bouquet of roses and a smile, shot by an American
But yours is here and yours is now
Grinning thickly on your Instagram
How nice.

Your soulmate isn't a starman from Mars
Or pretending he's from Venus
Not stillborn, not misdirected nor torn
They are not with some other woman or bloke

Writing verse in admiration; words so oddly bespoke
They did not try, fail and die, years before your time
On some other side of the planet
Self-sabotaged in synonyms of seclusion
Because they simply couldn't stand it
No, of course not.

Your soulmate is alive and he's
Beside you, presently
Forevermore
It's astonishing to me
Just how lucky you are.

LIVERPOOL

With you, I've never seen
A day without the sun
For you are a poem, or an encore
Just before another one
You are eyes that soliloquise
And give quote and verse wise, in time.
You're not my birthright nor my home
But you just make sense
For you are the present
Through the lens of the past tense
From Edge Hill to Wavertree
There's community, courage and bravery
And your shadow always seems
To catch up with me.

You are the relief of a deep breath
I hear security in your voice
I feel a rebellion in the air
In both silence and in noise.
You are lively, varied and spiky
With roads that lead to the sea – and they invite me
To ponder my thoughts and love them
You are a grandfather with wisdom
A smile and a trick up his sleeve
A caring remedy to tears and grazed knees
And with you, I've never seen
A day without the sun
Liverpool, you just seem to know
Something that I don't.

FROM HEAVEN TO ST HELENS

There was a chance, for a few hours
I could return to heaven
But by Wednesday morning
You were back in St Helens.

There was a hope, I thought
For communication and new dedication
But before I could muster the words
You were at the train station.

There was a prospect of respite
But again, you appeared in my dreams
That seems like a peculiar place
For you to be.

THE LIGHTS ARE OFF, BUT SOMEBODY'S HOME

Idiosyncrasy is dead but
Two and a half glasses blur the lines
To become the philosopher
That many generations have left behind.
Let's go to Barcelona in September
We'll drink Madri by the cathedral
We'll walk in circles and love one another
And drown out all evil.

Ignore the lights of the nightlife and hear
The words the bands badly sing
And you'll find out pretty quickly
Life is just impossible to live.
And in the mutters from the crowd
You can feel the sickness and distaste
Towards the ageing men on stage
Without a pretty face, since 1988.

Nuance is dead and
The singer refuses to move with the times
He's the type who'll get jet-lagged
From a forty-five-minute drive.
The least funny part was when
He told a joke, though the encore was good
For a moment, it looked like skill
But most certainly, it was luck.

On these nights, caution is a double-edged sword
And that's the trouble with two-pound pints
Bubbles and thrift are such a dangerous mix
You'll see the light, by quarter to nine.
And even with all the time in the world; with a million guesses
You'll never again find Isabella and
Don't you ever put two and two together
Because you might get four.

Faces turn pale with ale and whisper something to the extent of
One day, all of our heroes will be dead
Just like the rest, the evening drifts towards history
And to me, the social world remains the great mystery
Because life is so much simpler on your own
The lights are off, but somebody's home.

MUSIC IS YOUR ONLY FRIEND

Music is your only friend
It's far too late
To deny this or otherwise pretend.

Music is the only thing
Deep down, that you care about
Even just a little bit.

Don't use your imagination or trouble your mind
Because I know you'll discover
So much that you don't like.

Instead, music will vocalise your cries
Forcefully reveal all that you conceal
And hold you close at night.

Music is the saviour, as it's
The only thing that makes any sense
On this wasted planet.

What will follow your five seconds of fame?
Headaches, mistakes and sertraline
Voices with malice will beckon your name.

Instead, music will stir and lure you
Proudly it will rouse and vow
To help you see the real you.

Because music says all that you truly want to
And not just what you're supposed to
Music articulates, with grace
The everyday disappointments on your face
It cuts through the noise
Of the ordinary boys.
Leave your bags at the door
To say, there is no more
In this sphere, the despair, the fear
Is your duet
And daily, it'll remind you
So that you never forget
That music is your only real friend
And who even cares
If the world will soon end?
Music will guide you as you live
And stay with you when you're dead.

JIMMY'S A SINGER

Jimmy's a singer
And underneath it all, you'll find
An authentic human being
Who's caring, decent and kind.

Jenny carries a tote bag and an ambivalent face
A knee graze and a lifelong malaise
She sups bottles at the weekend
And does shots on weekdays.

Jimmy's a winner
In five seconds, from ant to aeroplane
With eyes that are so heavy
With regret and with pain.

Lauren's a waterfall
She plays the game and she's not ashamed
By her Chelsea boots, her hatred of men
Her pint of Amstel, or her German girlfriend.

Jimmy's a sailor
And he sneers at Martha and Vivian
Downright jealous of their prescribed trajectory
Of oblivious to oblivion.

Daisy's a blessing
She does lines to pass the time, to overcome the worst

She's so sharp and so quick that around her
I worry I might burst.

I hadn't seen Jean
Since I was fifteen
She didn't know the places I'd been
Or the things I'd seen.

Jimmy's a singer
And above all else
He'd just like the world to see him
As he sees himself.

Jimmy was a friend of mine
And despite everything
I loved him,
For a time.

HIGH TOWN

Six o'clock waits for me with anticipation
With art, assurance and self-emancipation
Light is a stencil.

Dusk is an inviting enigma
That reveals many things in sedating winter
There are no answers.

Modern defeats… victories, are so small
Yet I fear and revere and feel them all
Every inch. All is temporary.

I am here, hands elegant, legs intact
Breath flowing, heart attacked
Present, despite all circumstance. That

I am here – I never had a choice
To adopt this skin, this face, this life, this voice
Young man, you don't know what you're missing.

A debut of stillness, peacetime lives
Somehow. My God, I hope heaven is
Half as good as this.

The rain saunters to the windscreen and I wonder
If my life will ever come to
Anything useful.

IF YOU WERE A TWIN

If you were a twin
And the two of us met with an embrace
Could we put aside and reject
The distaste of a familiar face?

If you were a twin
Would you want to meet me?
Open to receive, folded in the bath, could we grasp
The joy of new beginnings?

If I was renewed
And if you were a twin
Could something good work?
Would I feel something?

And could we dance to the music
In all manner of movements
In the same way the film stars do it?
If you were a twin.

PLEASE READ TO ME

I think I've been premature about summer
My fixations can often wane and fade for others
I wanted love that was true and a life holistic
I learnt when I was six years old, that was unrealistic
So, so much for summer
So much for the summer.

Connection is whittled and crafted, and almost never discovered
This is the fiction, the fallacy of fathers and mothers
And time and again I feel the need
To stow some slippery trick hidden up my sleeve
To combat the numbness of all I see and feel.
Oh, how I wish I was real.

When you are too a ghost, will I still encompass
My philosophy of fixation and lust for purpose?
A magnetism to salvation and to have you nearby
When all is lost and again the once new day has died
And I can no longer see,
Will you, please read to me?

I hold in my beaten hands, the fruits of nothing
While trees across campus are starting to blossom
With patience to stretch, snap and break like elastic
I revere and bow to you, the last glimmer of the fantastic
Evening; don't leave.
Please read to me.

THE BRAIN GONE STALE

I'm sick of shit conversation
And days wasted
I miss my medication.

I miss drink and fun
And the sobering sun
I miss being in love.

I miss being able to write
And being able to sleep through the night
I miss when I didn't
Know quite so much.

I miss creating something that I
Truly believe in
I miss the feeling

Of things feeling right
Nothing has felt right
For such a long time.

WHEN I GET BACK FROM THE FUNERAL

When I get back from the funeral
Will you hug me?

Will you hear my sighs, straighten my tie
And try your best to love me?

When there's rain all the way
Through July, will you see it through with me?

When I'm grimly sipping pineapple and whisky
Will you look past or see me?

I hope you will.

I hope you see the irony
In the positive things I sometimes say.
I hope that sometimes you'll think of me
When I go away.

I don't know where to begin
And so, I won't.
But I hope you'll try to learn and to get to know
Each of the tomorrows I've borrowed.

I hope so.

Will you comfort me
When I am resigned and, once again, retired?

Will you know all that roams beneath
When my face is stoic, but tired?

Will you let calming resolution
Become the routine and the usual?

Will you hug me
When I get back from the funeral?

THINK OF ME

Think of me
As the west and as the east.
Think of me
As seminal, famous or as obscurity.

Think of me, if you're lonely or
If you're bored.
Think of me as the answer
To no question at all.

Think of me
As quiet and madness
Think of me
As pathos and sadness.

Think of me, infrequently
As seasick
Think of me, fondly
As one who died and then lived.

Think of me as once safe in arms
With a purpose, and with drive – so bizarre.
Think of me as once a crutch
In friendship and in love
Who am I now?

Think of me as all I could have been
And as the portrait of your face that grins in my dreams.
Think of me as lost and found
And again lost
What have I now?

Think of me as what could have been
Think of me as the things they've never seen
Think of me as lost and found
Think of me as lost.

Think of me as I was yesterday
Think of me as you sleep
Think of me as the west
And as the east.

ME AND A FRIEND OF A FRIEND

I am her, just the same as
She is me
She is a squeeze of ease and spontaneity.

Her twenty-year plan, stands and exists
Just for her to stay exactly as she is
And truly, I believe her.

Every week she finds – to call home – a new place
And still she, only ever wants to escape
But whatever, I could never
Free her.

When she beams towards me I
Slightly melt; I cannot hide my smile
For I live through her.

I saw our demise in a dream, one night
And I screamed to her in my sleep
I am you, just as you
Are me.

SHAKE A SPEAR, MY WAY

Sight. Stole me first, in a cavern
Of hesitation; you were light.
Empty and devoid of religious faith
Or of any other smite.

Hear. From afar, and curiosity
Builds – for what is near.
Wonder. I am reigned in
Seasick; before strain or blunder.

Smell. And life is no longer… for
It is fantasy, not here nor hell.
Touch. And existence is not real
It is too much.

Concern. And I am a transformed
Animal, home fires burn.
I feel more, absorb more, change
Analyse, I read your face. I learn.

20ᵗʰ MARCH

It is six years since
I danced with Blanche Dubois
I was captured by her brunette make-believe allure
And I was a homesick chalet girl.
I remember well, the steady smell, the excitement of youth
I'm still the same, I feel this everyday - always
This lure of the unobtainable, the pull of everything fictitious
I'm older now – I understand mostly, what is mine what isn't.

Four years ago, the whole world closed
And I saw the river clean
On the precipice of viewing a side of Blondie
That I had never before seen.
And not again seen since
Her dance was unholy, her rhythm was free
And never again would she look
The way on that night, she looked at me.

About two years ago I conquered the world
Or so my mind seems to tell me and to recall
Ma familia, so unfamiliar
Memories dropped like fallen heroes, platitudes all.
It's strange how the horizon can change
The bar edges higher

The present can never quench
New expectations, of ancient desires.

I wasn't made to last
Yes, hello, I stand alone
In a way that's both self-assured and fragile
All life is a hypnotic tangle, much simpler spent alone.

I am here and I am also still there
In equivalent measure, in equal share
Time changes all and leaves little suggestion
That it was ever there.
Time attacks and buries your body, leaving no evidence
That we were ever there.

IN THE END THERE WILL BE SILENCE

In the end there will be silence
Serenity and rest will come your way,
If these walls could talk
They wouldn't have much to say.

With the end will come reflection
As blunt and as sober as a sunrise,
Modern lovers shall become one another
Try to not worry so much, it'll be alright.

After peace has ceased, and too has violence
In the end there will be silence.

When the last man sleeps, with faded heartbeats
The riddles of the universe will be known
The world is so much bigger than you and
It's ok to leave some things alone.

When the speech has been spoken
There'll be a happy never after,
A swarming storm of nothing and
An end to all these disasters.

After the heartbreak, finally, sense will commence
Besotted empty bottles and 8pm danger,

We all embark on the melancholy mission
Of stranger to stranger.

After peace has ceased, and too has violence
In the end, my friend, there will be silence.

When the curtains are drawn, there will be solitude
And that is all, so goodnight.
When the door closes, there is only you
To dissipate and become one with light
And that is all, so goodnight.

SI SOLO, AMIGO

On your eve
Please excuse my slight unease
I'm not so used to this mix
Of dusk and company – but please…

If I am to run out of words
Forgive me, it has happened once or twice.
For you, I'd give all of them up
I know your place, in my life.

Funerals are for the living. Somewhere along the line
The dead felt just the same
And all that we had
Surely, remains.

Please don't mind the present time
Understand, in the face of catastrophe and disaster
If I could write my future
You'd be in every chapter.

WHAT'S THE SECRET?

Going back
To the past
Is really quite easy
If you know
The right sunsets
To follow.

And, trying again
Just like before – it won't last
Soon you'll realise
Just as I have, and as I do
That no one ever comes
To save you.

YOUR WEDDING DAY

˚

You put on your dress, and your eyes confessed
The meaning behind all of this mess
You are my home and I
Cannot find you.

You looked past the cake, and you gave
A glance of contempt my way
And speaking as one who's quite familiar
With that particular feeling…

Do you think you might've been
A little unfair on me?
I remember when we were we
I know far too – much of you.

Your remaining days will attempt
To break your arms and burn your legs
Test you to the edge and render you mad
And yet still, over me, you'd rather have that.

Your wedding day
This year has been a thousand miles
Outside of my comfort zone
Here, it's always Christmas.

Your wedding day
I wrote the same song

Every day for twelve years
And by the end I was bored to tears
I love you, but...

I can't remember the tired lines
I fed to you, in the Bridal Room,
But they don't seem
To have meant very much to you
I never believed it could be us
But I suppose I hoped
It might be different.
I hate you, but...

If it all goes wrong
I'll be there – somewhere
If you lose your very last friend
I'll be around,
Somewhere.

ANOTHER DAY

You fight
So very hard
Only, to be
Kicked down
Twice as hard
And…
They tell you
On the television,
In books
Through misjudged
And idled looks
You are… what's wrong
The issue and
The problem.

They said
Obsession was a curse
Addiction, a disease
Oh, please.
They are lifeboats
Charms of refuge
Booze and wide-hearted schemes
Are an escape from bad dreams
Keep-me-a-floats
To brake slightly
Rebel, just lightly
Against this tumultuous, nauseous

Slipping landslide
Of time.

We say
The same words
In different ways
The pit of stomach sadness
That has carried us
Through life… is symmetrical
You and I
We're the same.
And so, into
Onto
In-front-ta
Another day
We go.

Say goodbye now and
Don't you dare wake me
Tomorrow, as you go
I don't think I could face
Another truth
Quite so soon
I sleep with my hands
Behind my back
For I – cannot stand
The thought of forwards
Forewords
Or further murder
Yet, onto… another day
I go.

NEW YEAR'S EVE

I don't think I've ever heard silence
Not properly.
My teeth stay clenched, my back hunched
Brain ineffective; mind dizzy
Waiting for a word, any message
Of salvation from my
Unguarded heart.

Misinformation is a saturated market
And I have been had
Time and time again.
Life's various punctuations
Are always, always killers
Alysha, to live
Is such a peculiar thing.

With Jools Holland and a final sunset
New Year's Eve is truly
A taste of your own death.
Night invites you to ponder
Time renders your soul tender
And when you try so hard to forget
All you can do is remember.

SHANE MACGOWAN

Shane MacGowan dies and I
Fall apart again. Into pieces remembering
A snarled lip, rhythmic hip
And our fond memories of him.

Tumble dried and fried by time
Shane authentically knew struggle and he knew pain
Yet he plunged on, not a single fuck he gave
Let his legacy lead the world – follow his ways.

Shane MacGowan
Another of the gang, crunched
Maybe someday in heaven
We'll meet up for lunch.

Shane MacGowan dies
And I am in pieces again, bereft
With all of God's mercy
May he now safely rest.

IF I WERE TO DIE

In every moment, I can feel myself eroding
As I forget the shower of loving eyes upon me
I gesticulate towards empty seats and slowly
The myth, the curse, all inevitable… becomes reality.

If I were to go, if I were to die
I could be no longer forgotten
No longer bitter, jealous, twisted nor rotten
Just, free.

Each day that passes, I can feel myself succumbing
To these sedimentary narratives
And even now, after all laughs, tears, declaratives
There shall be no fairytale.

So, tell me again
How we are spinning tornados
Destined to be safe together.
I have lived my life as a fool and to you
I don't even slightly deny it.
In the face of decisions, I could've made
I dwell, I swim, I yomp in shame
I'm getting every ounce
Of what I deserve.
I just cannot bear to be alone
Any longer.

If I were to dwindle, if I were to die
I would be no longer crushed
By waves twice hourly, nor dropped or lost
By those who once adored me.

If I were to be swayed, if I were to die
Maybe, my love
We could come back here in the spring
And lie together, under the sun.

EVE

It's growing dark outside and
Eve is asleep on my arm
She's had a long day, and so have I
Her mother is dead and I'm not sure
If she's noticed yet
I'm talking aloud and
Nobody's listening.

I do have brief moments where I genuinely believe
It all might be ok
I suppose it's these little delusions that
Give tomorrow life; prevents our extinction
And delays the end of us.
These fairytales only exist in my head
Existence is purely about perspective,
Nobody's listening.

Eve ignores it but
She knows my morals have gone
Stealing, cheating, freewheeling
My standards have left me and I
Feel nothing of the evil I've become.
It's always such a shame to think what might have been.
Nobody's listening.

Her sleeping eyes recognise, that there was a time
The world began to crumble; dystopia ensued
And I loved it. I devoured it, I ate it… I kissed it.

I stood at the top of a mountain, and I screamed.
I often wonder how long that time really lasted
A month? Four months? More?
It can't have been much longer than that
My memory is so uncertain and obscured. There was a time
I would die at the reflection of any slight misdemeanour
There was a brief spell when I controlled the world.
And if you can believe it,
I was a human being.

These were the days when our dreams
Still belonged to us.
They still meant something.
Now, a blank canvas – an empty page
Does not strike fear, is no longer a challenge nor opportunity
But a still… nothingness.
And truthfully, I die each time
I journey to the reservoir of my mind, so thirstful
Almost lustful. Just…
Desperate…
And I come back dry
I return on my own.

Eve is asleep on my arm
For both her and I, tomorrow
Will be almost impossible
My eyes do not focus as they once did
They saunter, hazed, blinking in nothing but hope
The artist has been buried; the human perished
Life is a moment, death a permanence
I am a watercolour and I've had to wash away
I didn't want to. Honestly.

ODE TO ZOPICLONE

The legs are first to go
It is then you are safe, and you know
Refuge shall come soon.
Hands heavy, hands slow.

Me and Juliet wish we'd never met
And the shining light amidst all of this regret
Is the silence of the mind that
Edges my way.

By quarter past nine
Begins the race against time
Pioneering occasion! Quirky situation!
Victory is mine. I can only win.

For a stupor must commence
It has set off, it's on its way
And here on God's finest day
You can revolt and turn and say
Enough! Enough!
Nada! Nada! Basta!
No more of this disaster!
Enough! Enough.

Mouth dry and my dilated eyes spy
Ceiling, the darkness – goodnight.
Goodbye.

I'll miss you, little guy.

FOR YOU

I've met you for the very last time
On about eighteen occasions now
You are a fairytale, one that lingers for all time
Now that lemon and rhyme has passed me by, I distress at how…

I am damned to stay grounded, without you
Without a break from earthquakes; just like heaven
No refuge nor new news. Just. Silence.
…eerie disappearance.

I've wondered for a while now, how long before
He becomes I? Blood orange in my eyes, I despair; I apologise for hurting you
And for becoming many things
I promised not to.

And promises have come too easily, not few nor far between
They slipped from my tongue too carelessly; now found out, stout and old
I lie in the ruin of mistruths, your absence, and who we could've been
Look after yourself, tortured soul.

You were a moment in time
One that I'm struggling so much to set free
I do believe that, in a different world
We could have conquered the planet – you and me.

HIDE AWAY

I'm just one more goodbye from
Complete collapse, and as I scale – move along
This planet, I find – I must rewrite and alter my desires
More times than the history of a liar.

So, I'm going to hide away, I think you understand
How time has twisted my gut and
How I've become the skeleton whose artistic merit dies
In the sunken-eyed skull of a nine to five.
I'm going to hide away, for I am perpetually seasick
And if push comes to love, I'll be anyone
You need me to be. Before the line I,
Owe to you that much.

I'm only one hello from being free
I've had the oddest week – you must by now believe me
I was resigned to blur and to cross lines, and never again
Say anything, of any real consequence.

So, I'm going to hide away, because you can change
What – but not who you are, and in some ways
Finding what you love and letting it kill you
Has eaten me alive.
I'm going to hide away, and for you
I'd have been anyone
I had to. So, thank you,
You've been so kind, but I must go.
I stood square in the face of the tide, and I smiled
But the tide has won.

*"Though your sins be as scarlet,
they shall be as white as snow."*
                                          Isaiah 1:18

ABOUT THE AUTHOR

Hailing from West Yorkshire, England, Jacob Davies possesses a unique poetic mind which best expresses and articulates itself through the written word, words he was seemingly born to write. His work is sharp and to the point, but also draws on the abstract and largely unseen from everyday, real-life situations.

His poetry resonates with people who see and reflect on the inherent sadness in the everyday. Jacob has an ability to express and shine a light on those complicated thoughts that lurk in the back corners of the mind.

The Dream Must Die is his third and boldest collection to date. It offers both a growing maturity, heightening his challenge to today's societal norms, whilst at the same time reflecting the ruthless struggle against the recognition of one's fate and the unwinnable war against time. His poems drip with empathy, conflict and loss as he continues to wrestle with the human condition, contemporary society and its contradictory positions of love, hate, acceptance and prejudice. He is both at peace and at war. His work is both uncomfortable and comforting. He sees the individual in the crowd and when you absorb his work you feel seen, heard and noticed personally and individually.

His work has received critical acclaim from inception and his readership continues to grow due to his ability to articulate ostensibly hidden everyday thoughts in such a poignant and echoing way. Whilst he cites Anne Sexton, Christina Rossetti, Morrissey and Oscar Wilde as influences, Jacob reaches new audiences and new corners of consciousness with his pioneering and contemporary work.

Jacob regularly writes articles for various publications, such as the *Morrissey Mercury* and *Yorkshire Arts & Minds*, has edited several published poetry collections and is a regular songwriter for Franco Rivers.

He often performs across the UK to share his work and to meet with his readers.

Jacob performing at The Queen's Mill, Castleford, August 2023.

www.JDVSWriter.com

This book is printed on paper from sustainable sources managed under the Forest Stewardship Council (FSC) scheme.

It has been printed in the UK to reduce transportation miles and their impact upon the environment.

For every new title that Troubador publishes, we plant a tree to offset CO_2, partnering with the More Trees scheme.

MORE TREES
LET'S PLANT A BILLION TREES

For more about how Troubador offsets its environmental impact, see www.troubador.co.uk/sustainability-and-community